I0006097

UCN #43 Wireability of an Ultracomputer

Abstract

We analyze the wireability of an Ultracomputer, a shared-memory MIMD parallel machine with thousands of processing elements, wired using an Omega connection network. We show a way of structuring hardware involving large numbers of processors into smaller subsets of processors and switches. A design with 4096 processors, based on present-day wiring technology and electrical power considerations, is presented. This design assumes a 2x2 switch on a chip is available, also a 1 megabit memory chip and a high speed microprocessor chip with 32 bit addressing.

UCN #43 Wireability of an Ultracomputer

1.0 Introduction

This paper studies the wireability of a 4096 processor Ultracomputer. This is basically the task of wiring 4096 processors to 4096 memories, in a manner allowing any processor to communicate with any memory. A suitable interconnection network is required. The network we propose is composed of 2x2 switches, each designed on a single chip. Note however that this key chip has not yet been built. A central idea is to exploit the modularity and basic symmetry of the network design. To exhibit this modularity and symmetry the present paper will show several smaller and less complex versions of the network. These smaller networks will then be built up into a 4096x4096 design; a larger 64Kx64K design will also be described.

We begin by considering small structures since the immediate goal of our project at NYU is to produce an 8x8 prototype and then go on to a 64x64 machine. Basic design issues like backplane wiring, power, and reliability will be discussed. Our design does not assume any new breakthroughs in VLSI or interconnection technology. Everything presented can be implemented with today's technology, construed conservatively.

For related material see Gottlieb et al. [82] and the references therein.

4

2.0 Description Of Method

An n stage omega network (Lawrie [75], Goke and Lipovsky [73]) can be laid out utilizing many different topologically equivalent interconnection networks. One such is a network utilizing a "perfect shuffle" interconnection between each stage. While this yields a network which uses a single fixed wiring pattern between each of its stages, the wiring required becomes excessive as the number of stages increases. Instead we propose to use a variant of the "baseline" network (Wu and Feng [80]) shown in Figure 1, which involves a series of different interconnection patterns in successive stages but which leads to a more modular and manageable design.

A major advantage of the network shown below is that it can be split in the middle, yielding two symmetric halves. These halves can then be split in half again and then rejoined, using a two dimensional interconnection scheme. This results in a total layout involving only one challenging backplane, but very short, straight wires at all other points of connection.

The following observations can be made concerning the 16x16 network shown in Figure 1. After each stage the network splits into two identical parts, an upper half and a lower half. There are no connections between these halves for successive stages. One half of all the interconnections between stages are short, straight line paths. If we compare the two dimensional network shown in Figure 1 to the topologically equivalent 3D alternative shown in Figure 2, we see

5

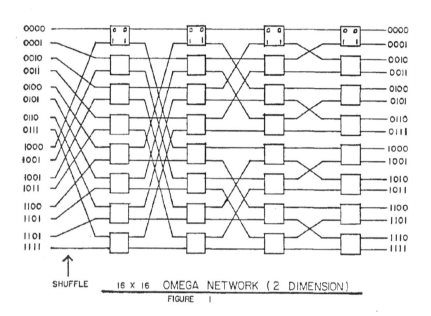

SHUFFLE   16 X 16   OMEGA NETWORK (2 DIMENSION)

FIGURE   1

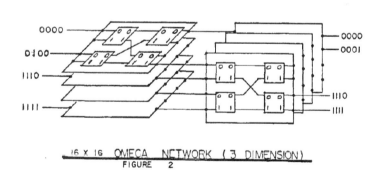

16 X 16   OMEGA   NETWORK   (3 DIMENSION)

FIGURE   2

6

that in Figure 2 the wires are far shorter. In the two dimensional network, some wires must cross past four switches, but in the three dimensional case at most one cross-over is needed.

A further observation is that if the network is constructed three dimensionally, as shown in Figure 2, it can be split into two symmetric halves, laid out on planes which run perpendicular to each other. In this configuration, the interface between the two halves uses very short, "straight through" connections only.

The key to this treatment of the network lies in the way in which the three dimensional orientation of the two sets of switch boards is handled. In both the 16x16 case shown in Figure 2 and in the 64x64 case shown in Figure 3, just the amount of wire needed to connect two adjacent switches together is used at the interface between two sets of boards turned at right angles to each other. As the overall system increases only the length of wire on each board increases. In the larger case, the lengths of one (additional) column of the wires on the new larger boards double, but the rest remain the same length as before (Figure 3).

Another important attribute of a three dimensional network is the fact that it is composed of smaller building blocks. The two dimensional network of Figure 1 is implemented on a single board using 32 switch chips. The corresponding three dimensional network (Figure 2) is implemented with eight much smaller boards of only four switch chips

7

$$64 \times 64$$

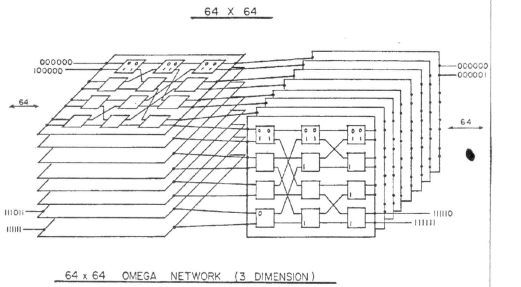

64 x 64   OMEGA   NETWORK   (3 DIMENSION)

FIGURE   3

each. The maintainability of the three dimensional network is therefore better since if a switch fails, a replacement of a smaller and less costly board is possible.

The rationale of the three dimensional networks shown in Figures 2 and 3 is as follows: The total data motion function of this network can be separated into two suboperations where the first half of the problem is to route data to any line in the correct target group of output lines and the second is to route the data within a group. In a 16x16 structure there will be 4 groups of 4 lines each; in a 64x64 structure, 8 groups of 8 lines each. In the 16x16 case, the horizontal boards route the input data to one of four output boards. This means that each input board needs only to route its data to the correct one of four output boards. This is done by grouping output ports according to the high order data destination address bits. Once the data is routed to a particular output board, the output board must then select which one of the four output ports the data is to be routed to. This effectively breaks the problem into two halves. The critical advantage of this method (first described by Wise [81]) is that the boards can be placed orthogonally to one another in such a way that each port of the four input boards is adjacent to the port on one of the four output boards corresponding to the connection described above. Thus all the wires between boards are short "straight through" connections.

Similarly, if an 8x8 network is implemented on a card, 8 cards can be connected orthogonally with 8 other cards creating a 64x64 switch (Figure 3). The central cross-section through which all wires pass along straight lines can be thought of as a grid of rows and columns. A point (processor) on a row board can select any column (middle), and the point on the corresponding column board (middle) can then select any row (memory). Therefore there exists a unique path from any point (processor) on one side, to any point (memory) on the other side.

3.0 A 4096 PE Design Based On 64x64 Blocks

Starting with the 64x64 switch described in the previous section, and constructing an array of 8 by 8 of these switching blocks on one side, and a second 8 by 8 array of like units on the other side, we are again presented with two ends and a middle (Figure 4). However the middle interconnections can no longer be a series of "straight through" wires since the 64x64 blocks with which we must work present a two dimensional square face. If this physical structure is adopted, one must wire in a way which brings the face of each of the 64x64 units to a unique row of this middle section for the left half group of 64x64 units, and each face of the 64x64 units on the right side to a unique column of the middle section. These rows and columns can then be wired straight through. The requirement necessary to wire the square face of each 64x64 block to a unique row or column is that the area for connections remain the same. Therefore, the area of the square face of connections for each 64x64 block must be equal to the

10

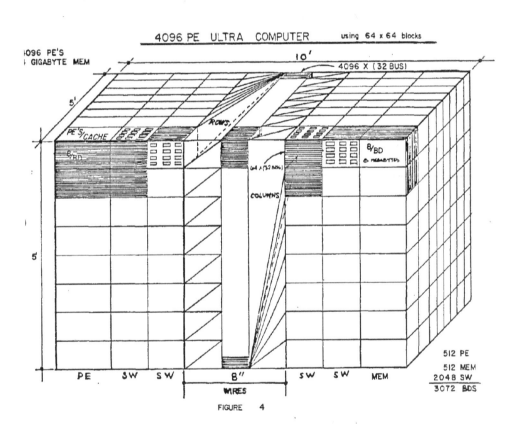

FIGURE 4

11

area of the linear rectangular row or column.

To determine the wireability of this configuration we present an alternate, more easily visualized, wiring scheme. We remove the center section (labeled WIRES in Figure 4) and rotate the remaining two pieces so that the cut faces are forward. The resulting geometry is shown in the top of Figure 5. We treat these two faces as a backplane to be wired with a wire connection grid of 100 pins per square inch and a wire packing density of 500 wires per square inch. To accommodate 32 connections per switch port, 4096 ports, power, and ground the required size of each half of the backplane is approximately five feet by five feet. Since there are 4096 x 32 wires between the two halves, the combined cross section of these wires is approximately 250 square inches. Distributing these wires evenly over the five foot height yields a buildup of four inches of wire. If we fold these two halves back a middle thickness of eight inches would result. The described scheme uses wires for interconnections. If a printed circuit board is developed for these interconnections, at least an order of magnitude smaller width will result.

The important parameters in wiring this configuration are wire lengths and buildup. A scheme with a shorter maximum length and smaller buildup is shown in the bottom of Figure 5. Here the wire buildup has been reduced from four inches to three inches, while the maximum wire length has been reduced from 11.2 feet to 9 feet. To minimize the average wire length and buildup, the prosessors (PE's) and memories

12

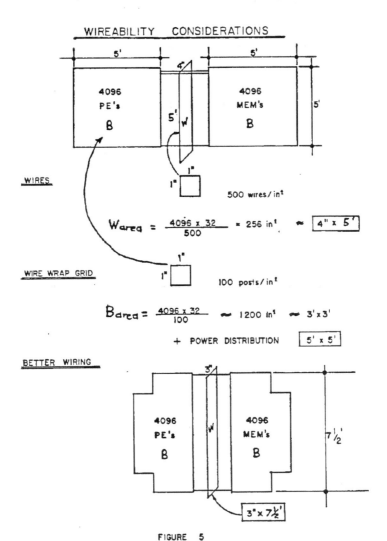

WIREABILITY   CONSIDERATIONS

WIRES

$$W_{area} = \frac{4096 \times 32}{500} \approx 256 \text{ in}^2 \approx \boxed{4'' \times 5'}$$

500 wires/in²

WIRE WRAP GRID

100 posts/in²

$$B_{area} = \frac{4096 \times 32}{100} \approx 1200 \text{ in}^2 \approx 3' \times 3'$$

+ POWER DISTRIBUTION $\boxed{5' \times 5'}$

BETTER WIRING

$\boxed{3'' \times 7\frac{1}{2}'}$

FIGURE   5

13

(MEM's) can be intermixed as shown in Figure 6. An optimal solution may be obtained by placing the faces of the backplane parallel to each other as shown in Figure 4, but wiring the ports directly without intermediate rows and columns. Recall that each face consists of an 8 by 8 array of blocks, each containing a sub array of 8 by 8 ports. We must wire each block to all 64 blocks on the other face by connecting Port(i,j) in Block(k,l) of one face to Port(k,l) in Block(i,j) of the other face. With this design it may make it difficult to repair faulty connections.

Smaller Ultracomputer configurations are shown in Figures 7 and 8. A 64K processor Ultracomputer (see Figure 9) can be configured in much the same way as a 4K Ultracomputer. This processor requires a 16x16 network card and a larger wired backplane. Note also that the size of the backplane in a large Ultracomputer configuration can be reduced significantly, but with some loss of performance, by using some appropriate serial system of data transmission, or buses for either rows or columns.

4096 PE ULTRA COMPUTER STRUCTURED AROUND A BACKPLANE

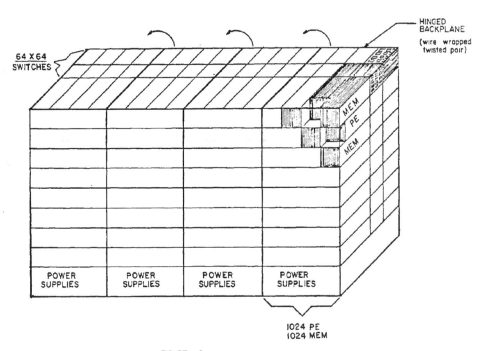

FIGURE 6

15

FIGURE 7   8 PE "ULTRA"

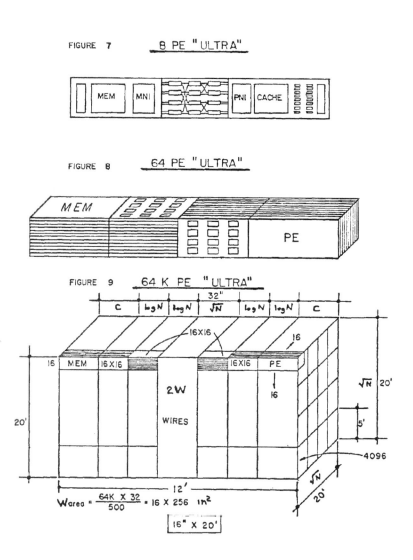

FIGURE 8   64 PE "ULTRA"

FIGURE 9   64 K PE "ULTRA"

$$W_{area} = \frac{64K \times 32}{500} = 16 \times 256 \ in^2$$

16" X 20'

4.0   Ultracomputer Boards For 64x64 Blocks

4.1   Processor Board

For the basic 64-processor block shown in Figures 3, 4, and 6, an 8 processor PE board is needed (see Figure 10). This would contain 8 microprocessors, each with a large address space (32 bit address, 4 gigabyte).   Hardware for high speed floating point operations is also desirable. An important op-code that the processor must support is the Fetch and Add operation described in Gottlieb et al, which is essential for effectively coordinating an array of multiple processors. A memory management unit (MMU) should also be included on the PE board and, because of the poor latency characteristic of a large Omega network, a cache is appropriate, e.g., an associative cache of set size 2, block size (cache line) 32 bits and 16K byte capacity and special microprocessor op-code functions (Flush, Write through, etc.).

A processor network interface (PNI) must be included on the board. For this 32 connections are assigned per processor in the configuration shown. (Messages consisting of data and address are broken up at this interface into 32-bit packets for transmission over the switch network. These 32 bits are time multiplexed between input and output.) Also considered is an area on the board for I/O service and diagnostics with a serial I/O connection.

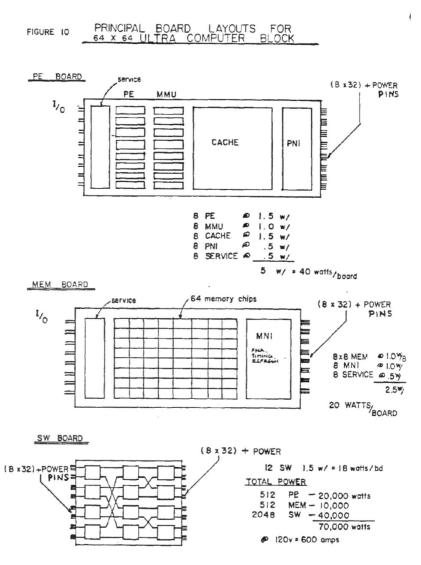

FIGURE 10 PRINCIPAL BOARD LAYOUTS FOR 64 x 64 ULTRA COMPUTER BLOCK

PE BOARD

service

PE MMU

I/O

CACHE PNI

(8 x 32) + POWER PINS

8 PE @ 1.5 w/
8 MMU @ 1.0 w/
8 CACHE @ 1.5 w/
8 PNI @ .5 w/
8 SERVICE @ .5 w/

5 w/ = 40 watts/board

MEM BOARD

service 64 memory chips

I/O

MNI

FNA. TIMING REFRESH

(8 x 32) + POWER PINS

8 x 8 MEM @ 1.0 w/8
8 MNI @ 1.0 w/
8 SERVICE @ .5 w/

2.5 w/

20 WATTS/BOARD

SW BOARD

(8 x 32) + POWER PINS

(8 x 32) + POWER

12 SW 1.5 w/ = 18 watts/bd

TOTAL POWER

512 PE — 20,000 watts
512 MEM — 10,000
2048 SW — 40,000

70,000 watts

@ 120v = 600 amps

18

The board needs roughly 8x32 pins, plus power on one side and a few pins on the other side of the board for serial I/O.

4.2 Memory Board

The memory board shown has eight independent memory arrays (Figure 10). It is assumed to utilize megabit chips organized to supply several bits per access. With the projected availability of 256K memory chips by the end of this year, such a chip might be available within three years. A memory network interface which implements the fetch and add operation and a 32-bit alternate ("back-end") I/O path is included on this board. Timing and refresh logic must also be included. A service area which provides an alternate means of reading and writing each memory array is shown.

The assumed capacity of this board is one megabyte per module or eight megabytes total capacity plus error correcting logic. The edge connector of this board should be designed so that a PE board could connect directly to this board to produce eight independant processors with memory. This combination could be useful for maintenance and could serve as a front end peripheral processor array.

The memory board has 8x32 pins on the side that connect to the switch board. The other side of the board can be used for back-end I/O and diagnostic functions.

19

4.3 Switch Board

The switch board design assumes a single chip 2x2 switch and therefore requires 12 chips for its 8x8 switching function (Figure 10). The interconnection between columns of the 2x2 switch could be as shown in the figure or could be a "perfect shuffle". The 8x32 edge connections on both ends must satisfy two conditions. They must be able to plug directly between a PE board and a memory board and must also connect orthogonally with each other so that 64x64 switch array can be formed. A possible additional feature to the board could be a line driver/receiver pair at the final backplane connection.

The 2x2 switch chip, whose structure is outlined in Gottlieb et al, queues and routes packets in the forward and reverse directions. The chip also combines requests directed at the same memory location and "uncombines" memory responses to combined requests. Note that to combine Fetch and Add an adder must be included in each chip.

5.0 A 4096 PE Design Based On A 64x64 Arrangement Of Planes

The design of a 4096 PE Ultracomputer without a backplane is possible (Figure 11). It requires the layout of a large board (plane) containing 3 stages of 32 2x2 switches and some longer wires between stages. The interconnection between the three stages on this board continue the "baseline" network. In addition to this board the previously described boards are used. Based on the previously discussed wireability factors, the board would be approximately five

20

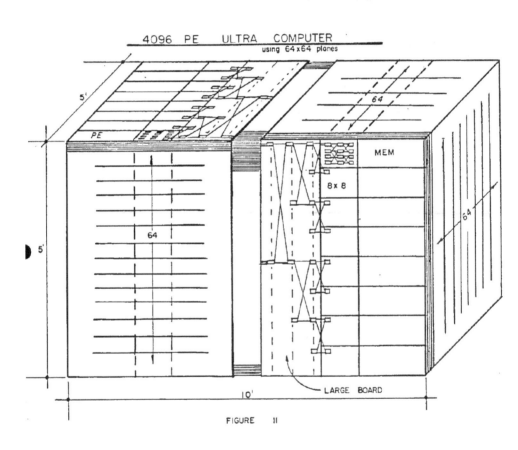

4096 PE ULTRA COMPUTER
using 64x64 planes

FIGURE 11

feet by one foot. When connected to 8 of the 8x8 switch boards, this board yields a 64x64 switch on a plane. Connecting 64 such planes to 64 orthogonal planes, while adding PE's to one end and memories to the other, results in a 4096 PE Ultracomputer with no backplane.

In addition to the lack of a backplane, an advantage of this layout is the shorter maximum length of wire per stage. In the other design we had small wire lengths up to the middle section. Here we distribute the length of the middle section among the stages on the large board. A disadvantage of this system is its need of a large board and possible physical difficulties connected with replacement of this board.

6.0 Some Remarks On Power Dissipation And On Reliability

The following is an estimate of power consumption for a 4096 PE Ultracomputer built out of the processor, switch, and memory boards described, assuming today's technology (see Figures 4 and 10). The processor board will consume about 40 watts per board. The memory board will consume about 20 watts per board. (Both of these boards contain chips that are presently utilized in air cooled systems.) The switch board is estimated to consume 18 watts. This estimate assumes a 2x2 switch chip designed with the same technology and packaging as the processor chip. Such a chip would require about 100,000 transistors, which is also about the same contained on the processor chip. Assuming that it is packaged in the same way as processors and

))memory, this chip could also be air cooled. (However, other technology and packaging may have greater cooling requirements.) The total power required for the logic would be about 70,000 watts, since 512 processor, 512 memory, and 2048 switch boards are required. Such a configuration can be air cooled; for greater densities of boards and smaller volume other cooling techniques might be required.

Maintenance of such a design is facilitated by the fact that the number of different system components is small (three). Reliability of the system is most critically dependent on the reliability of the switch chips. The memory modules should present few problems since they are error correcting and can function with inoperative chips. The processor boards can execute individual diagnostics periodically and report malfunctions. The switch network should be implemented using parity or check sums on messages and retransmissions. The total number of 2x2 switches required is approximately 25,000. Therefore, the mean time between failures should be long. If only one switch is down the system can be operated in a reduced configuration. If a switch adjacent to either a pair of memories or a pair of processors fails, only those two memories or processors are unavailable. In the worst case, if the failure is near the center of the network, the number of processors or memories that cannot be used is at most the square root of the number of processors. Network diagnostics must be developed and designed to isolate switch failures.

UCN #43 Wireability of an Ultracomputer

If each group of 8 boards in the 64 PE Ultracomputer (Figure 8) is augmented with a 9th board, or if each group of 64 boards in the 4096 PE Ultracomputer (Figure 11) is augmented with a 65th board, reliability can be greatly improved. The additional (9th or 65th) switch, processor, and memory boards would run diagnostics and sequence themselves in and out of the configuration, signaling the presence of inoperable components when these are detected. Implementing this idea requires a simple "active" backplane incorporating an additional common bus as illustrated in Figure 12. This backplane makes it possible to switch boards in and out of the Ultracomputer, and also connects the disconnected boards to the common bus. When one memory board is switched out of the system and another is switched in, the contents of the memories on the disconnected memory board must be copied to the memories on the connected memory board. The same applies to the cache on the processor board as well as a further requirement that the full state of the displaced processors must be copied to their replacements.

The procedure of substitution can be accomplished periodically by halting the processors allowing the network traffic to subside, and then effecting the exchange. The displaced processor, switch, and memory boards will then execute diagnostics, and upon sucessful completion will continue the exchanges in a preplanned sequence. These sequential exchanges would have the affect of rippling diagnostics through all of the components of the system. Upon detection of an error the defective component can be isolated out of

24

"ACTIVE" BACKPLANE
(FOR N² PE ULTRA COMPUTER)

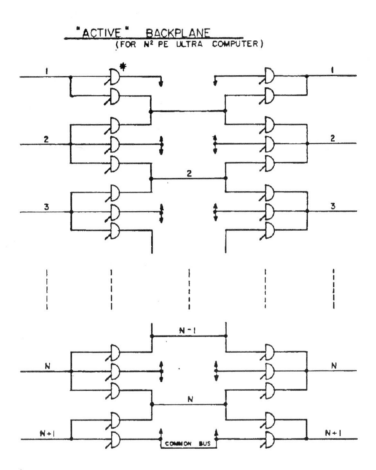

* NOTE: ALL GATES TRI STATE OR EQUIVALENT

FIGURE 12

the Ultracomputer and replaced when convenient.

Note that a similar technique can be used on each of the 64 processor board sets used in a 4096-processor system: a 65th processor can be provided in this group, together with the capability of switching out any processor of the group. This additional redundancy should give quite high reliability. The main remaining reliability exposure is in the functioning of the switch-in/switch-out circuits themselves, and if necessary an appropriate "majority logic" design can be used for this part of the overall architecture.

7.0 Summary

We have snown a novel technique for the modular wiring of an Ultracomputer based on the use of a 2x2 switch. A prototype of this hardware to be developed and built at NYU will provide insight to the specifications of larger switches, processor designs (with Fetch and Add, cache and processor network interface), and memory designs (larger size, with timing and memory network interface).

We expect technology to make lower power and higher wiring densities available in the next few years, so that machines like the Ultracomputer which we have described should be entirely feasible. A just as great, or greater challenge will be in the area of operating systems, compilers and algorithms. Computer applications must be studied with emphasis towards parrallel algorithms for execution. The

26

existence of a sufficiently large and interesting Ultracomputer will challenge software and algorithm designers to move vigorously forward toward these goals.

www.ingramcontent.com/pod-product-compliance
Lightning Source LLC
LaVergne TN
LVHW012201040326
832903LV00003B/40